BRITISH RAILWAYS STEAMING THROUGH THE SIXTIES

Volume Sixteen

Compiled by
PETER HANDS

DEFIANT PUBLICATIONS
190 Yoxall Road
Shirley, Solihull
West Midlands

Printed on behalf of Richard Netherwood Limited, by Gorenjski tisk d.d., Slovenia.

CURRENT STEAM PHOTOGRAPH ALBUMS AVAILABLE
FROM DEFIANT PUBLICATIONS

VOLUME 14
A4 size - Hardback. 96 pages
-178 b/w photographs.
£14.95 + £1.50 postage.
ISBN 0 946857 40 7.

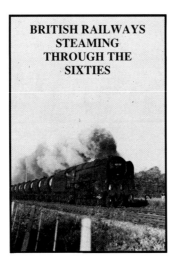

VOLUME 15
A4 size - Hardback. 96 pages
-178 b/w photographs.
£16.95 + £1.50 postage.
ISBN 0 946857 52 0.

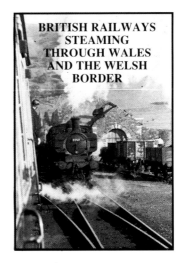

A4 size - Hardback. 96 pages
-175 b/w photographs.
£17.95 + £1.50 postage.
ISBN 0 946857 56 3.

VOLUME 1
A4 size - Hardback. 96 pages
-177 b/w photographs.
£14.95 + £1.50 postage.
ISBN 0 946857 41 5.

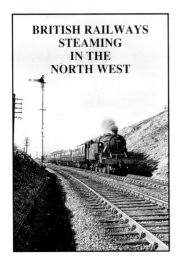

A4 size - Hardback. 96 pages
-174 b/w photographs.
£18.95 + £1.50 postage.
ISBN 0 946857 60 1

BRITISH RAILWAYS
STEAMING
IN THE
SOUTH WEST

IN
PREPARATION

VOLUME 11
A4 size - Hardback. 96 pages
-176 b/w photographs.
£16.95 + £1.50 postage.
ISBN 0 946857 48 2.

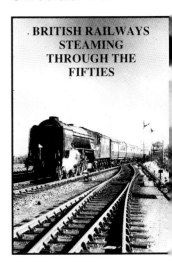

VOLUME 12
A4 size - Hardback. 96 pages
-176 b/w photographs.
£16.95 + £1.50 postage.
ISBN 0 946857 49 0.

VOLUME 1
A4 size - Hardback. 96 pages
-177 b/w photographs.
£14.95 + £1.50 postage.
ISBN 0 946857 39 3.

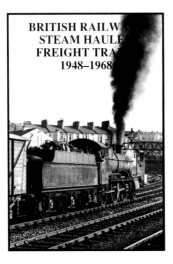

VOLUME 1
A4 size - Hardback. 96 pages
-174 b/w photographs.
£14.95 + £1.50 postage.
ISBN 0 946857 42 3.

BRITISH RAILWAYS
STEAMING
THROUGH THE
MIDLANDS

IN
PREPARATION

VOLUME 2

VOLUME16
A4 size - Hardback. 96 pages
-178 b/w photographs.
£18.95 + £1.50 postage.
ISBN 0 946857 61 X

FUTURE STEAM PHOTOGRAPH ALBUMS
AND OTHER TITLES

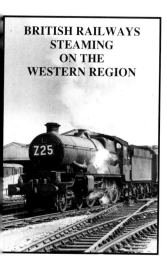

BRITISH RAILWAYS STEAMING ON THE WESTERN REGION

VOLUME 4
A4 size - Hardback. 96 pages
-177 b/w photographs.
£15.95 + £1.50 postage.
SBN 0 946857 46 6.

EARLY AND PIONEER DIESEL & ELECTRIC LOCOMOTIVES OF BRITISH RAILWAYS

A4 size - Hardback. 96 pages
-177 b/w photographs.
£15.95 + £1.50 postage.
ISBN 0 946857 45 8.

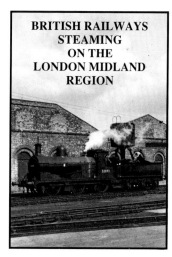

BRITISH RAILWAYS STEAMING ON THE LONDON MIDLAND REGION

VOLUME 4
A4 size - Hardback. 96 pages
-177 b/w photographs.
£15.95 + £1.50 postage.
ISBN 0 946857 47 4.

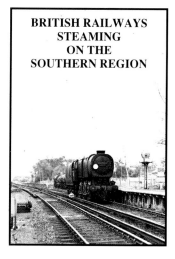

BRITISH RAILWAYS STEAMING ON THE SOUTHERN REGION

VOLUME 3
A4 size - Hardback. 96 pages
-177 b/w photographs.
£17.95 + £1.50 postage.
ISBN 0 946857 54 7.

BRITISH RAILWAYS STEAM HAULED TITLED TRAINS

A4 size - Hardback. 96 pages
169 b/w photographs.
£16.95 + £1.50 postage.
SBN 0 946857 51 2.

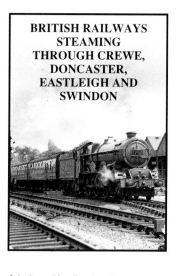

BRITISH RAILWAYS STEAMING THROUGH CREWE, DONCASTER, EASTLEIGH AND SWINDON

A4 size - Hardback. 96 pages
-179 b/w photographs.
£17.95 + £1.50 postage.
ISBN 0 946857 53 9.

BRITISH RAILWAYS STEAMING THROUGH LONDON

A4 size - Hardback. 96 pages
-174 b/w photographs.
£17.95 + £1.50 postage.
ISBN 0 946857 55 5.

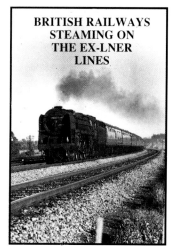

BRITISH RAILWAYS STEAMING ON THE EX-LNER LINES

VOLUME 4
A4 size - Hardback. 96 pages
-183 b/w photographs.
£17.95 + £1.50 postage.
ISBN 0 946857 57 1.

BRITISH RAILWAYS STEAMING FROM 1948–1968

'50th' ALBUM
A4 size - Hardback. 96 pages
186 b/w photographs.
£16.95 + £1.50 postage.
SBN 0 946857 50 4.

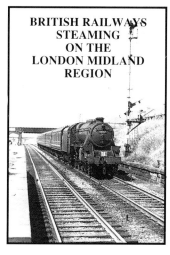

BRITISH RAILWAYS STEAMING ON THE LONDON MIDLAND REGION

VOLUME 5
A4 size - Hardback. 96 pages.
- 177 b/w photographs.
£17.95 + £1.50 postage.
ISBN 0 946857 58X.

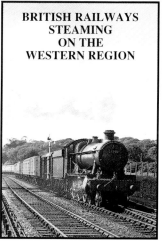

BRITISH RAILWAYS STEAMING ON THE WESTERN REGION

VOLUME 5
A4 size - Hardback. 96 pages.
- 177 b/w photographs.
£17.95 + £1.50 postage.
ISBN 0 946857 59 8.

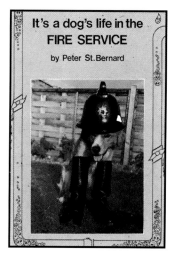

It's a dog's life in the FIRE SERVICE
by Peter St.Bernard

COMEDY
269 pages. Cartoons.
£9.95 + £1.00 postage.
ISBN 0 946857 30 X.

ACKNOWLEDGEMENTS

Grateful thanks are extended to the following contributors of photographs not only for their use in this book for their kind patience and long term loan of negatives/photographs whilst this book was being compiled.

T.R. AMOS
TAMWORTH

P.A.BRIDGMAN
HUCCLECOTE

B.W.L.BROOKSBANK
MORDEN

N.L.BROWNE
ALDERSHOT

R.BUTTERFIELD
MIRFIELD

R.S.CARPENTER
BIRMINGHAM

BRIAN COATES
SALISBURY,
NEW BRUNSWICK, CANADA

KEN ELLIS
SWINDON

TIM FAREBROTHER
BOURTON

CHRISTOPHER FIFIELD
LONDON

M.GASCOYNE
HIGH WYCOMBE

J.D.GOMERSALL
SHEFFIELD

B.K.B. GREEN
WARRINGTON

T.HAILES
OULTON BROAD

RAY HARRIS
NEW MALDEN

R.W.HINTON
GLOUCESTER

H.L.HOLLAND
ST.CATHERINES,
ONTARIO, CANADA

F.HORNBY
NORTH CHEAM

A.C.INGRAM
WISBECH

R.G.B.JACKSON
KEMPSTON

H.N.JAMES
IPSWICH

ALAN JONES
BATH

D.K.JONES
MOUNTAIN ASH

A.F.NISBET
BRACKLEY

T.B.OWEN
CAEMELYN

R.PICTON
WOLVERHAMPTON

W.G.PIGGOTT
UNKNOWN

N.E.PREEDY
GLOUCESTER

K.L.SEAL
ANDOVERSFORD

J.SCHATZ
LITTLETHORPE

C.P.STACEY
STONY STRATFORD

M.S.STOKES
MARPLE

J.M.TOLSON
BIGGLESWADE

S.TURNBULL
KIRKINTILLOCH

A.WAKEFIELD
DRONFIELD

D.WESTER
*

G.H.WILSON
SOLIHULL

MIKE WOOD
BIRMINGHAM

* Courtesy of the Norman Preedy collection.

Front Cover - With steam in its death throes in the Manchester area, begrimed heavy freight workhorse LMS Class 8F 2-8-0 No 48529 is a visitor to Heaton Mersey from 8A Edge Hill (Liverpool) on 6th April 1968. With clouds of smoke erupting from its chimney, No 48529 accelerates towards the camera with a lengthy mineral train. Drafted to 9D Newton Heath the following month, No 48529 was condemned from there in June 1968. (J.M.Gascoyne)

ISBN 0 946857 61 X

© P.B.HANDS 1997
FIRST PUBLISHED 1997

INTRODUCTION

BRITISH RAILWAYS STEAMING THROUGH THE SIXTIES - Volume Sixteen is the sixteenth in a series of books designed to give the ordinary, everyday steam enthusiast of the 1960's a chance to participate in and give pleasure to others whilst recapturing the twilight days of steam.

In this series, wherever possible, no famous names will be found, nor will photographs which have been published before be used. The photographs chosen have been carefully selected to give a mixture of action and shed scenes from many parts of British Railways whilst utilising a balanced cross-section of locomotives of GWR, SR, LMS, LNER & BR origins.

As steam declined, especially from 1966 onwards, the choice of locomotive classes and locations also dwindled. Rather than include the nowadays more traditional preserved locomotives in the latter days of steam, the reader will find more locomotives of SR, LMS & BR backgrounds towards the end of the book.

The majority of photographs used in Volume Sixteen have been contributed by readers of Peter Hands series of booklets entitled "What Happened To Steam" & "BR Steam Shed Allocations" (both still available) and from readers of the earlier "BR Steaming Through The Sixties" albums. In normal circumstances these may have been hidden from the public eye for ever.

The continuation of the "BR Steaming" series etc., depends upon you the reader. If you wish to join my mailing list for future volumes and/or feel you have suitable material of BR steam locomotives between 1948-1968 and wish to contribute them towards this series and other albums, please contact:-

Tel No.   Peter Hands,
0121 745-8421   190 Yoxall Road,
          Shirley, Solihull,
          West Midlands B90 3RN

CONTENTS

NAMEPLATES - Nameplate examples of the main representatives of British Railways.

1) GWR *Hall* Class 4-6-0 No 4909 *Blakesley Hall*. (N.L.Browne)

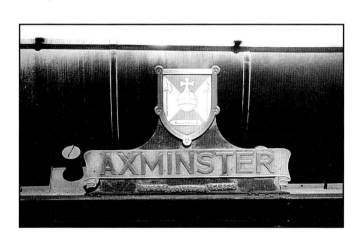

2) SR Rebuilt *West Country* Class 4-6-2 No 34018 *Axminster*. (D.K.Jones)

3) LMS *Jubilee* Class 4-6-0 No 45699 *Galatea*. (T.B.Owen)

4) LNER A3 Class 4-6-2 No 60066 *Merry Hampton*, (N.L.Browne)

5) BR Class 5 4-6-0 No 73112 *Morgan le Fay*. (D.K.Jones)

6) It is either an 'Open Day' or an official visit to Derby by an enthusiasts club on 14th June 1960 where there is a marked difference in the cleanliness of the front end and smokebox door of BR Class 9F 2-10-0 No 92107 which is a visitor to Derby shed (17A) from 15A Wellingborough. No 92107 took its leave of Wellingborough depot in December 1961, moving to a new abode at 21A Saltley. It also served from 2D Banbury, 1A Willesden and 8H Birkenhead. (G.H.Wilson)

) The SR H15 Class 4P5F 4-6-0's were a mixture of designs and rebuilds by Urie and Maunsell introduced between 1914 and 1927 and were utilised on many forms of traffic on the South Western Division of the Southern Region. In March 1960, No 30474 (71A Eastleigh) is noted at Southampton next to an unidentified SR M7 Class 0-4-4T. Condemned from Eastleigh shed the following month, No 30474 was scrapped at Eastleigh Works two months later. (R.S.Carpenter)

3) Bathed in warm sunshine former Robinson Great Central Railway 04/7 Class 2-8-0 No 63721, from 9G Gorton, is noted at rest in the shed yard at 6F Bidston in June 1960 next to a BR Class 9F 2-10-0. Upon closure of Bidston shed in February 1963 its final allocation was as follows:- LMS Class 2F 0-6-0 Tanks Nos 47160 and 47164, LMS Class 3F 0-6-0 Tanks Nos 47343, 47495, 47622, 47628 and 47674 along with BR Class 9F 2-10-0's Nos 92045-47 and 92165-67. (D.K.Jones)

9) With steam to spare, Derby Works constructed LMS Class 5 4-6-0 No 44810, of 21A Saltley, passes Defford aerodrome to the north of Cheltenham with a Birmingham bound excursion in the summer of 1960. Costing £ 9,500 to build in October 1944, No 44810 was one of 842 units to be built and examples could be seen at work from locations as far apart as Brighton and Wick. Transferred to 5D Stoke in March 1965, No 44810 was condemned from there in August 1966. (Tim Farebrother)

10) The fireman climbs down from the footplate of 84E Tyseley based GWR 5100 Class 2-6-2T No 4172 as the driver eases his charge towards the stock of a Worcester bound local passenger train at Malvern Wells station in the summer of 1960. Constructed by British Railways in 1949, No 4172 remained on the books at Tyseley shed until June 1963, moving to a final home at 84F Stourbridge. Withdrawn in January 1965 it was scrapped three months later. (Tim Farebrother)

1) 75A Brighton allocated SR Unrebuilt *West Country* Class 4-6-2 No 34019 *Bideford* heads a lengthy line-up of former Southern Railway engines in the shed yard at 71A Eastleigh in October 1960. Built in December 1945, *Bideford* spent the latter years of its twenty-two year career based at 70E Salisbury, 70B Feltham, 70D Eastleigh and 70A Nine Elms. It survived in revenue earning service until March 1967, being cut up later in the year at Cashmores, Newport. (R.S.Carpenter)

12) Smoke drifts lazily from the funnel of War Department Class 8F 2-8-0 No 90304 as it rests between duties outside its home shed at Mexborough in March 1960. This former Great Central Railway depot, coded 36B from 1949-1958 and 41F from 1958 until complete closure on 2nd March 1964, boasted a huge allocation of this class of locomotives. No 90304 moved to pastures new at 34E New England in November 1961, ending up finally at 40E Colwick in June 1962. (N.E.Preedy)

13) Its paintwork glistening and copper gleaming in the sunshine in the works yard at Swindon, 82D Westbury based GWR *Hall* Class 4-6-0 No 4945 *Milligan Hall* is fresh from overhaul in May 1960 and is awaiting fuel and water prior to returning to its home depot. Later in 1960, October, *Milligan Hall* was drafted to 81A Old Oak Common where it remained until March 1961, moving the short distance to 81C Southall from whence it was withdrawn later in the year. (N.E.Preedy)

14) Looking in fine external fettle, locally allocated (34A) LNER A4 Class 4-6-2 No 60026 *Miles Beevor* backs out of Kings Cross terminus light engine after bringing in an up express in August 1960. Constructed at Doncaster Works in 1937, *Miles Beevor* was originally named *Kestrel* (carried later by LNER A1 Class 4-6-2 No 60130). Modified with a double chimney in August 1957, No 60026 was transferred to the Scottish Region (64A St.Margarets) in October 1963. (N.E.Preedy)

15) Leaving a murky trail of exhaust in its wake, SR Unrebuilt *West Country* Class 4-6-2 No 34038 *Lynton* speeds through Clapham Junction station with an excursion on 24th September 1960 a month before being transferred from 72A Exmouth Junction to 75A Brighton. *Lynton* remained at Brighton shed for just over twelve months before returning to the South Western Division at 71A Eastleigh. A final transfer in December 1964 took it to 70A Nine Elms in London. (D.K.Jones)

16) From a Johnson design, first introduced into service during 1875, former Midland Railway Class 2F 0-6-0 No 58175 looks unkempt and bedraggled as it stands in the shed yard near to the massive concrete coaling plant at 18A Toton in May 1960 two months after being transferred from 16A Nottingham. Despite its shoddy external appearance, No 58175 managed to soldier on at Toton until December 1961, being cut up at Derby Works in February 1962. (D.K.Jones)

17) In marked contrast to the locomotive in the previous photograph, former North British Railway J37 Class 0-6-0 No 64632 looks in splendid condition in a section of the large yard at its home shed at 65A Eastfield (Glasgow) in March 1960. For the spotter on foot, Eastfield was a twenty minute walk from the nearest station at Cowlairs. On the occasion of the author's first visit in August 1962 there were forty-eight steam engines to be seen. (N.E.Preedy)

18) BR Class 4 4-6-0 No 75034 heads an express from the Chester direction at Shrewsbury in May 1960. At this date in time, No 75034 was itself a Chester (6A) engine. Later in its relatively short life-span, it was also based at 6K Rhyl (twice), 6B Mold Junction, 6G Llandudno Junction, 2B Nuneaton, 21D Aston, 5D Stoke and 10A Carnforth. After condemnation from the latter in February 1968 it was despatched four months later to Wards, Inverkeithing for cutting up. (N.E.Preedy)

9) During the summer months double-heading of holiday expresses with all types of locomotives being pressed into service from various parts of the Western Region were common sights at Birmingham (Snow Hill). One such combination glides into Snow Hill station from Wolverhampton with an express bound for South Devon in July 1960. Piloting an unidentified GWR 4300 Class 2-6-0 is GWR *Castle* Class 4-6-0 No 4098 *Kidwelly Castle*, from 83A Newton Abbot. (R.S.Carpenter)

20) All of the Stanier LMS 3-cylinder Class 4 2-6-4 Tanks, Nos 42500-36, were allocated to Shoeburyness shed, coded 13D and 33C during BR days, for use on the London Tilbury and Southend line and were employed in the main on the frequent passenger services to and from Fenchurch Street. The vast majority, like No 42523, seen in the yard at 33C in October 1960, were withdrawn in June 1962 upon the completion of electrification and scrapped at Doncaster Works. (N.E.Preedy)

21) Designed by Holmes and first introduced into service in 1882 the former North British Railway Class Y9 0F 0-4-0 Saddle Tanks were primarily involved in shunting duties in dockland areas and from time to time were hired to outside contractors. By January 1957 their numbers had been reduced to just eighteen, including No 68104, seen here at 64A St.Margarets (Edinburgh) in February 1960. Condemned in October 1962 it was cut up at Cowlairs in September 1963. (N.E.Preedy)

22) Looking somewhat self-conscious, the driver of GWR *Hall* Class 4-6-0 No 4933 *Himley Hall* stands near to his charge as it stands on the turntable at 71G Weymouth on 1st September 1960. *Himley Hall*, a visitor from 82D Westbury, was transferred to 82B St.Philip's Marsh in November 1962. Later transfers took it to 84E Tyseley (June 1963) and 6D Shrewsbury (September 1963). It died at the latter in August 1964 and was scrapped two months later. (Mike Wood)

3) In a flurry of white smoke and steam, SR Unrebuilt *Battle of Britain Class* 4-6-2 No 34086 219 *Squadron*, from 73A Stewarts Lane, climbs the one in one hundred incline out of Maidstone whilst powering an up boat train in August 1960. Once of 74B Ramsgate, *219 Squadron* had found its way to 73A by February 1958 via 72A Exmouth Junction and 74C Dover. It was ousted from Stewarts Lane for good in May 1961, returning to Exmouth Junction again. (Brian Coates)

4) On a dull-looking 15th March 1960, work-stained LMS Class 4F 0-6-0 No 44226, of 21A Saltley, awaits departure from the long gone Gloucester (Eastgate) station with a local passenger turn bound for Birmingham (New Street). Saltley shed had a host of these locomotives on its books, used in the main for freight services and banking duties on the Camp Hill line. No 44226 was withdrawn from Saltley in September 1964 and Eastgate was closed in 1975. (Tim Farebrother)

25) A small cluster of enthusiasts gather near to the footplate of smartly turned out 86G Pontypool Road allocated GWR 4300 Class 2-6-0 No 5306 which is providing the power for an RCTS special at Cheltenham (St. James) station (closed in 1966). The trip on 10th September 1961, encompassed a tour of the now long-defunct Midland and South Western Junction line. Despite its vintage, No 5306 survived in service until June 1964, being withdrawn from 87A Neath. (N.E.Preedy)

26) The concrete coaling plant dominates the background at 21A Saltley on 17th September 1961. Lurking beside the plant is an unidentified BR Class 9F 2-10-0. The main subject matter is locally based LMS Class 4F 0-6-0 No 44520 which is in charge of a rake of flat wagons. No 44520, a longstanding inmate at Saltley, was condemned from 1A Willesden in January 1964. The coaling plant remained in situ long after the shed closed to steam in March 1967. (N.E.Preedy)

27) Sunlight and deep shadows at Tonbridge station on 20th June 1961 where begrimed BR Class 4 2-6-4T No 80038, recently transferred to the local shed (73J) from 73F Ashford, is in charge of a vintage coach. No 80038 was one of a large batch of these engines which were transferred to the Southern Region from the LMR in November 1959. It ended its days based at 83D Exmouth Junction, being taken out of revenue earning traffic in September 1964. (D.K.Jones)

28) LNER J69 Class 0-6-0T No 68549 is smartly turned out as it stands in light steam in the yard of its home shed at 30A Stratford on 17th March 1961 in the company of another local inmate, LNER N7 Class 0-6-2T No 69714. Dating from 1902, No 68549 was the product of a design by J.Holden for the Great Eastern Railway and had a working life of some sixty years upon withdrawal in February 1962. It was cut up at the nearby workshops. (N.E.Preedy)

29) With an ex.works Bulleid Pacific in the background, SR M7 Class 0-4-4T No 30031, newly allocated to 71B Bournemouth from 70B Feltham, displays its new coat of paint as it stands next to a sister engine in the yard at 71A Eastleigh on 4th February 1961 following an overhaul at Eastleigh Works. Once of 75A Brighton, No 30031 worked from Feltham shed for a number of years before moving to Bournemouth, where it was destined for withdrawal in May 1963. (T.R.Amos)

30) Despite being constructed by British Railways in 1948, Peppercorn inspired LNER A2 Class 4-6-2 No 60539 *Bronzino*, fitted with a double blastpipe and chimney, had a relatively short life-span of only fourteen years when withdrawn from 52D Tweedmouth in October 1962. It is seen here departing from York and heading homewards to 52B Heaton in August 1961 with a Leeds to Newcastle express via the coast route. After withdrawal *Bronzino* was stored at 52C Blaydon. (N.E.Preedy)

31) Bright sunshine envelopes GWR 1366 Class 0-6-0PT No 1369 at Weymouth on 24th September 1961. Designed by Collett and first coming into service in 1934, the class was restricted to just six units, several of which were a common sight through the streets of the town with boat trains. No 1369, along with sister engines Nos 1367/68 were transferred to 72F Wadebridge in August 1962. After withdrawal in November 1964, No 1369 was preserved on the Dart Valley Railway. (D.K.Jones)

32) On 11th February 1961, GWR *Hall* Class 4-6-0 No 6902 *Butlers Hall* (82C Swindon), seen here at 81D Reading later in the month, was involved in a serious accident on the Great Central main line to the north of Rugby when it collided with derailed northbound wagons of a freight train. *Butlers Hall* was thrown on its side, sustaining major damage, and the driver was fatally injured. Three months later the authorities condemned No 6902 and it was cut up at Swindon. (T.Hailes)

33) With a new tower block, a sign of the affluent sixties, rising in the left of the frame, the now long since preserved SR *Schools* Class 4-4-0 No 30925 *Cheltenham*, from 70D Basingstoke, backs onto its train at Waterloo in September 1961 after having travelled light engine from 70A Nine Elms. For many years a 73B Bricklayers Arms steed, *Cheltenham*, was transferred to the South Western Division a month before this picture was taken, from 73A Stewarts Lane. (N.E.Preedy)

4) Fowler LMS Class 6P5F 'Crab' 2-6-0 No 42933, of 2B Nuneaton, is noted light engine at Tamworth (Low Level) on the West Coast Main Line during July 1961 when work on the overhead electrified lines had just commenced in the station area. No 42933 was drafted from Nuneaton shed to 5A Crewe (North) two months later. During its latter days of service it was allocated to 6A Chester (twice) and 6C Birkenhead prior to being taken out of service in May 1963. (N.E.Preedy)

5) The powerful Gresley designed LNER 02 Class 2-8-0's were designated purely for freight haulage and were exclusively allocated to the sheds at Doncaster, Grantham and Retford. In light steam in bright sunshine outside the former Great Central three-road straight running shed at 36E Retford on 27th August 1961 is home-based No 63926. Condemned from Retford in September 1963, No 63926 was scrapped at Bulwell Forest Wagon Works twelve months later. (T.R.Amos)

36) Complete with a tablet-catcher for working over the single Highland lines, 63A Perth based LMS Class 5 4-6-0 No 45483 is a visitor to the wooden-roofed shed at Stirling (65J) on a sun-filled 21st May 1961. Rendered surplus to the requirements of the operating department at Perth, No 45483 was drafted to 64C Dalry Road (Edinburgh) in October 1961. Its last home was at 64A St.Margarets (Edinburgh) from whence it was condemned in December 1966. (N.E.Preedy)

37) SR Unrebuilt *Battle of Britain* Class 4-6-2 No 34051 *Winston Churchill*, from 72B Salisbury, glides into Poole station, on the South Coast, with a lengthy Weymouth to Waterloo express in August 1961. Constructed in December 1946, No 34051 was a popular resident of Salisbury shed for many a year until being withdrawn for preservation as part of the National Collection in September 1965, several months after hauling the great man's funeral train. (N.E.Preedy)

38) Although built under the ownership of British Railways in July 1950 at Swindon Works, GWR *Castle* Class 4-6-0 No 7033 *Hartlebury Castle* lived for less than thirteen years despite being modified with a double chimney in June 1959 and only completed 605,219 miles during its short career. It was allocated to 81A Old Oak Common for most of its life and is noted at Exeter St.Davids station with a down express on 16th August 1961. (Christopher Fifield)

39) Tank engine power abounds in a section of the yard at the former Glasgow and South Western shed at 67A Corkerhill (Glasgow) in May 1961. Leading a trio of engines is locally based BR Class 4 2-6-4T No 80008 which is in splendid external condition. No 80008 spent all of its working life at Corkerhill, being condemned in July 1964. In the left of the picture is LMS Class 4 2-6-4T No 42124, a visitor to Corkerhill depot from 67D Ardrossan. (N.E.Preedy)

40) Kilwinning station, junction for the lines to Largs and Troon, is the setting for this shot of BR Class 4 2-6-0 No 76099, another 67A Corkerhill (Glasgow) steed, which trundles along in May 1961 with a short goods train. Drafted to England to 5D Stoke in January 1965 after spells at 67C Ayr, 67A Corkerhill (again) and 67D Ardrossan, No 76099 ended its days at 16B Colwick. Withdrawn in August 1966 it was scrapped at Cashmores, Great Bridge. (N.E.Preedy)

41) Leaving the landmark of the massive girder bridge in the background, LNER A3 Class 4-6-2 No 60083 *Sir Hugo*, from 52B Heaton, arrives at York station with a down express on 8th August 1961. Built at Doncaster Works in 1924, *Sir Hugo* was modified with a double chimney in August 1959 and equipped with German style smoke deflectors in February 1962. Transferred to 52A Gateshead in June 1963, *Sir Hugo* was condemned from there in May 1964. (D.K.Jones)

2) Paired with a straight-sided tender a rather less-than-clean GWR *Hall* Class 4-6-0 No 6901 *Arley Hall* is a visitor to 84F Stourbridge from 86G Pontypool Road where it is seen at rest in the yard on 17th September 1961. Once of 84K Chester (GWR), 86C Cardiff (Canton) and 87F Llanelly, *Arley Hall* had been at Pontypool Road since September 1959. Withdrawn in June 1964, No 6901 was stored at 86B Newport (Ebbw Junction) prior to scrapping in October 1964. (N.E.Preedy)

43) The SR C2X Class 0-6-0's were a Marsh rebuild of the earlier C2's and came into service in 1908. Despite their vintage the first inroads into the class with condemnations did not occur until 1957, with Nos 32434 and 32537 succumbing. From then on withdrawals were rapid and the class was rendered extinct by February 1962. A small number were allocated to 75E Three Bridges, including No 32529, seen in blazing sunshine on 16th September 1961. (B.K.B.Green)

44) Begrimed LNER K1 Class 2-6-0 No 61822, from 40A Lincoln, is pressed into service on an express seen here passing the site of the closed (1953) site of Murrow West station on former joint tracks of the Great Eastern/Great Northern Railways as it speeds towards Doncaster on a misty 11th August 1962. This was the last year of service for the surviving K1's and No 61822 was withdrawn in November 1962. It was scrapped at Wards, Broughton Lane, Sheffield in March 1963. (T.R.Amos)

-5) Young spotters take their notes as they amble around 75A Brighton on a bright 7th October 1962. In the left of the frame is an unidentified SR A1X 'Terrier' Class 0-6-0T whilst in the centre is locally based SR *Schools* Class 4-4-0 No 30923 *Bradfield*, destined for condemnation two months later. To the right of *Bradfield* is SR U1 Class 2-6-0 No 31891, a visitor to Brighton from 75E Three Bridges, which was withdrawn during March 1963. (B.W.L.Brooksbank)

6) We move from the South Coast to the heart of the West Midlands, where, on Christmas Eve 1962, there is a sprinkling of snow on the ground, the forerunner of the vicious winter of 1962/63. Under partially clear signals, LMS Class 5 4-6-0 No 45180, of 21B Bescot, rattles a pick-up freight through Wednesbury and heads towards Dudley. No 45180 remained at Bescot shed until April 1965, moving to 2E Saltley, five months prior to withdrawal. (T.R.Amos)

47) A fully coaled but unidentified WD Class 8F 2-8-0 hides behind an ex.works mineral wagon which is situated at an unusual angle within the shed yard at 34F Grantham in February 1962. The focal point of this picture is of LNER 02 Class 2-8-0 No 63941 which had been allocated to 34F since moving from 36A Doncaster in November 1961. These locomotives were a common sight in the Grantham area on the High Dyke iron ore trains until their demise in 1963. (N.E.Preedy)

48) Once of 81D Reading and 85B Gloucester (Horton Road), 81C Southall based GWR *Hall* Class 4-6-0 No 4989 *Cherwell Hall* is a visitor to 84G Shrewsbury on 21st October 1962. Between June 1963 and condemnation in November 1964, *Cherwell Hall* was subjected to four transfers - 86G Pontypool Road, 82D Westbury (July 1963), 83B Taunton (January 1964) and 86E Severn Tunnel Junction (October 1964). After a period of storage at 86E it was scrapped at Hayes, Bridgend. (J.Schatz)

49) Late summer sunshine beats down on a sparsely populated Basingstoke station where we espy 72A Exmouth Junction based SR Unrebuilt *West Country* Class 4-6-2 No 34033 *Chard* at the head of a Bournemouth line express on 1st September 1962. In common with all the surviving Exmouth Junction Bulleid Pacifics, *Chard* was ousted from there in September 1964, moving to 70D Eastleigh. After withdrawal in December 1965 it was cut up at Buttigiegs, Newport. (J.Schatz)

50) Following in the footsteps of former Midland Railway 'Big Bertha' 0-10-0 and LNER Beyer-Garratt Class 2-8-0+0-8-2 No 69999, BR Class 9F 2-10-0 No 92079 (equipped with a double chimney) established itself as a popular resident banker at 21C/85D Bromsgrove for many years. On 25th August 1962 it is banking the 1.58pm Bristol (Temple Meads) to Newcastle (Central) express up the Lickey Incline. The train engine is LMS *Jubilee* Class 4-6-0 No 45656 *Cochrane*. (R.Picton)

51) GWR *Castle* Class 4-6-0 No 7001 *Sir James Milne*, from 84A Wolverhampton (Stafford Road), powers its way through Priestfield (Monmore Green) station, closed in 1972, with an excursion on 8th September 1962. Once a longstanding resident of 81A Old Oak Common, No 7001 had been at 84A since September 1961. Constructed in May 1946 it was originally named *Denbigh Castle*, but was renamed in February 1948. It was condemned in September 1963 from 84B Oxley. (T.R.Amos)

52) Resident former London and North Western Class 7F 0-8-0 No 49361 is seen in the company of a sister engine in the lengthy yard at 21B Bescot on 16th April 1962. By the end of the year the class had been slaughtered by withdrawals leaving just three survivors, Nos 48895 (21C Bushbury), 49173 and 49361, both of Bescot shed. For some obscure reason all three managed to soldier on late into 1964. No 49361 was scrapped at Cashmores, Great Bridge in April 1965. (N.E.Preedy)

53) Having emerged from possibly its first major overhaul since being built in August 1958, BR Class 9F 2-10-0 No 92233, of 88A Cardiff (Canton) and equipped with a double chimney, waits in Swindon Works yard to be steamed and returned to its home shed on 21st January 1962. After later spells at 82F Bath Green Park and 86A Newport (Ebbw Junction), No 92233 was transferred to the LMR, serving from 9D Newton Heath, 12A Carlisle (Kingmoor) and 8H Birkenhead. (N.E.Preedy)

54) In pristine condition, LNER A1 Class 4-6-2 No 60116 *Hal O' the Wynd*, allocated to 52B Heaton, steams into Doncaster station under the watchful eyes of a railwayman with a Kings Cross to Leeds express on 13th July 1962. Two months later and *Hal O' the Wynd* was at a new home - 52D Tweedmouth, where it was employed on semi-fast expresses to and from Edinburgh until October 1964 when it was transferred to a final base at 52A Gateshead, being withdrawn in June 1965. (J.Schatz)

55) As withdrawals of steam engines increased in momentum in Scotland several 'dumps' were created, including one at Lugton. In store there on a wet autumn day in 1962 is LMS Class 2P 4-4-0 No 40621, withdrawn from 67A Corkerhill (Glasgow) in October 1961, along with several Corkerhill LMS *Jubilee* Class 4-6-0's. Although not officially condemned until December 1962, examples of the latter at Lugton consisted of Nos. 45621, 45665, 45707, 45711 and 45720. (R.Butterfield)

56) Modified with a double chimney in July 1958 and German style smoke deflectors in September 1961, 1925 built A3 Class 4-6-2 No 60059 *Tracery*, of 34A Kings Cross, passes Crescent Junction signalbox and steams into Peterborough (North) station with the 1.40pm Kings Cross to Leeds and Bradford express on 18th August 1962. At one time *Tracery* was allocated to 38C Leicester GC, moving to 34A in April 1957. It was withdrawn from there in December 1962. (B.W.L.Brooksbank)

57) During 1962 the lengthy branch line from Oxford to Fairford was closed and we bade farewell also to the intermediate stations at Cassington Halt, Eynsham, South Leigh, Witney, Brize Norton & Bampton, Carterton, Alvescot, Kelmscott & Langford and Lechlade. During the occasion of an enthusiasts special along the line on 16th June 1962, the weeds are taking over as 81F Oxford based GWR 5700 Class 0-6-0PT No 9653 takes refreshment in the yard at Fairford. (D.Webster)

58) Isolated in a section of the yard, SR Unrebuilt *West Country* Class 4-6-2 No 34002 *Salisbury*, from 72A Exmouth Junction, awaits attention at Eastleigh Works on a sunny 18th February 1962. Constructed in June 1945, *Salisbury* remained at Exmouth Junction shed until September 1964, moving briefly to a new abode at 70D Eastleigh. Three months later it was on the move again, this time to 70A Nine Elms from whence it was rendered surplus to requirements in April 1967. (J.M.Tolson)

59) The footplate crew are keeping themselves warm within the confines of their charge, GWR 2800 Class 2-8-0 No 3820 (81E Didcot) as it steams light engine over a boarded crossing at Oxford on 24th December 1962. Once of 84K Chester (GWR), 84C Banbury, 84B Oxley and 82B St.Philip's Marsh, No 3820 had been a Didcot steed since February 1961. It remained there until January 1965, moving to 81C Southall and condemnation six months later. (J.Schatz)

60) LMS Class 5 4-6-0 No 45017, from 8F Springs Branch Wigan, speeds along beneath 'the wires' at Acton Bridge on the West Coast Main Line with an up fitted express freight on 8th September 1962. Allocated to Springs Branch from 24L Carnforth in May 1959, No 45017 eventually moved on again in July 1963, this time to 27C Southport. It was destined to survive until the end of steam in August 1968 and was cut up at Drapers, Hull in May 1969. (B.W.L.Brooksbank)

51) With an electric pylon standing sentinel-like in the background, like some 'War Of The Worlds' monster, former North British Railway J35 Class 0-6-0 No 64510 is sidelined at Craigentinny in Edinburgh in September 1962. Although fully coaled, it is doubtful if this 64A St.Margarets (Edinburgh) locomotive ever turned a wheel in revenue earning service again. Withdrawn in November 1962 it was scrapped at Inverurie Works in May 1963. (N.E.Preedy)

52) One of a numerical sequence of such engines based at 70D Basingstoke, Nos 75075-79, BR Class 4 4-6-0 No 75076, fitted with a double chimney and paired with a larger capacity tender, stands on an ash disposal road at 70A Nine Elms on 17th March 1962. When Basingstoke shed lost its parent code status in March 1963, No 75076 was transferred to Nine Elms. In May 1965 it was drafted to Eastleigh shed, by then coded 70D, being withdrawn in July 1967. (N.E.Preedy)

63) BR Class 9F 2-10-0 No 92063 is temporarily stored along with two sister locomotives out in the open at 52H Tyne Dock on a sun-filled 28th September 1963. This depot was allocated ten of these engines, Nos 92060-66 and 92097-99, for working over the tortuous route from Tyne Dock to Consett with heavy iron-ore trains. All were either withdrawn or transferred away from Tyne Dock between June and October 1966. No 92063 was scrapped in April 1967 at a yard in Stockton. (N.E.Preedy)

4) With a member of the railway fraternity posing for the camera, LMS Class 5 4-6-0 No 44994, from 64C Dalry Road, has steam to spare as it gently blows off its safety valves within the spacious confines of Perth station after arriving with an express duty from the now long closed (1965) former Caledonian Railway station at Edinburgh (Princes Street) on 4th September 1963. No 44994, a longstanding inmate of 64C, was condemned in July 1964. (A.F.Nisbet)

5) Another locomotive with a longstanding association with a single depot was SR Rebuilt *West Country* Class 4-6-2 No 34040 *Crewkerne*, of 71B Bournemouth. *Crewkerne* is sited near to the turntable at 70A Nine Elms on 4th May 1963. On 27th April 1963, No 34040, along with sister engines Nos 34028/42/45/50/52/88/94 and 34098 were all seen at Birmingham (Snow Hill) with football specials from Southampton in connection with a semi-final of the FA Cup at Villa Park. (N.L.Browne)

66) As the footplate crew prepare to provide refreshment for their charge, an uncared for BR Class 4 2-6-4T No 80090 exudes plenty of steam at Dundee Tay Bridge's Platform 4 before coupling up to its local passenger train bound for Tayport on 3rd September 1963. Originally a Welsh and English based locomotive, at 6H Bangor and 6C Birkenhead, No 80090 had made the move to Scotland (62B Dundee Tay Bridge) in February 1960, surviving until March 1965. (A.F.Nisbet)

67) As passengers alight within the dark confines of the station, a driver chats to a colleague on the footplate of SR U Class 4P3F 2-6-0 No 31625, locally based at 70C, as it blows off excess steam at Guildford station with a cross-country Redhill to Reading service on 17th August 1963. No 31625, from a Maunsell design of 1928, was withdrawn from 70C in January 1964. After a lengthy period of storage at Barry Docks it was saved by the Mid-Hants Railway. (A.F.Nisbet)

58) After what was possibly its last major overhaul, LMS *Royal Scot* Class 4-6-0 No 46152 *The King's Dragoon Guardsman*, from 6J Holyhead, looks resplendent in a new coat of paint as it stands near to the paint shop at Crewe Works on 11th August 1963. Also ex.works is LMS Class 8F 2-8-0 No 48709, of 8D Widnes. *The King's Dragoon Guardsman* remained at Holyhead shed until January 1965, joining its few surviving colleagues at 12A Carlisle (Kingmoor). (T.R.Amos)

69) Bearing its Western Region numberplates, to all intents and purposes GWR 5700 Class 0-6-0PT No 5775 is ready to be steamed and returned to its home shed at 86G Pontypool Road on 28th April 1963 from Swindon Works after overhaul. But this was not to be the case. No 5775 was later re-admitted to the works and painted in the maroon livery of the London Transport Executive. Withdrawn in January 1970 it was preserved by the Keighley and Worth Valley Railway. (J.Schatz)

70) The former Raven designed North Eastern Railway Q6 Class 6F 0-8-0's were used almost exclusively on freight duties in the north-east of England and were spread around a multitude of depots on the North Eastern Region. Despite being first introduced into traffic in 1913 withdrawals did not affect the class until 1960 and some examples survived until September 1967. On 28th September 1963, No 63439 (52K Consett) heads a freight at Tyne Dock. (N.E.Preedy)

71) One of the last surviving working examples of the Drummond Caledonian Class 2F 0-6-0's (vintage 1883) looks in a forlorn condition next to a 2-6-4 Tank engine type in the yard of its home depot at 65J Stirling in June 1963. No 57261, transferred to Stirling shed in November 1962 after a lengthy sojourn at 65B St.Rollox, succumbed to the inevitable in November 1963. Following a long period of storage it was cut up in June 1964 at Campbells, Airdrie. (Ray Harris)

72) Looking fresh from shops, locally shedded (17A) BR Class 4 4-6-0 No 75056 is in steam hemmed in a line-up of locomotives in the snow-sprinkled yard at Derby Works on 13th January 1963. Included in the line-up is another BR Class 4 4-6-0, an LMS Class 3F 'Jinty' 0-6-0T and an LMS Class 8F 2-8-0. No 75056, built in March 1957, had been allocated to 16A Nottingham prior to being reallocated to Derby in September 1962. It was withdrawn in June 1966. (D.K.Jones)

73) Constructed by BR in June 1950, GWR *Castle* Class 4-6-0 No 7032 *Denbigh Castle* had an active working life of just over fourteen short years when taken (prematurely) out of revenue earning service from 81A Old Oak Common in September 1964. *Denbigh Castle*, modified with a double chimney in September 1960, is seen here speeding past Swindon Works with a parcels train on 28th July 1963. After withdrawal, No 7032 was scrapped at Birds, Risca in 1965. (N.E.Preedy)

74) The freight orientated depot at Toton (18A and 16A) was a huge affair with a number of large roundhouses to accomodate its massive allocation of steam engines. One such resident, BR Class 9F 2-10-0 No 92078, rests in bright sunshine with a sister locomotive on 7th April 1963. On the occasion of the author's last visit to the shed on 13th September 1965 there were just twenty locomotives to be seen, of which only eleven were in steam. (K.L.Seal)

75) By the end of June 1962 the once numerous Wainwright SR C Class 2F 0-6-0's were finished in normal everyday service, but there was a reprieve for three of them, Nos 31271/80 and 31592, which were employed as shunters at Ashford Works, eventually being taken into Departmental Stock. On a dull September day in 1963, No 31271 drifts through Ashford station light engine. Later used as a stationary boiler, No 31271 was cut up at Ashford in December 1967. (A.C.Ingram)

76) Once a longstanding member of the small fleet of LNER A4 Class 4-6-2's allocated to the 'Top-Link' shed at 64B Haymarket, No 60004 *William Whitelaw*, was drafted to 61B Aberdeen (Ferryhill) in June 1962, but returned to 64B from September 1962 until July 1963, moving back to Ferryhill again. On 15th April 1963, *William Whitelaw*, in shabby external condition, departs from Stirling with the 4.00pm express from Dundee to Glasgow (Buchanan Street). (J.Schatz)

77) More Pacific power, this time of the London Midland and Scottish Railway variety. Stanier *Coronation* Class 4-6-2 No 46225 *Duchess of Gloucester*, of 12B Carlisle (Upperby), rests between duties near to the running shed at 1B Camden in the summer of 1963, not long before the closure of the depot to steam. *Duchess of Gloucester*, allocated to Upperby from 5A Crewe (North) in July 1959, was rendered surplus to operating requirements in October 1964. (R.G.B.Jackson)

78) Nearing the end of its lengthy, but inauspicious career, LNER J50 Class 0-6-0T No 68922 looks suitably unkempt outside its home shed at 56A Wakefield on 21st July 1963. Withdrawn two months later, No 68922 was scrapped at Darlington Works. Near to No 68922 we can just make out the cab of LNER B1 Class 4-6-0 No 61131, another Wakefield steed, which had worked from a variety of sheds in the Bradford and Wakefield areas for much of its life. (N.E.Preedy)

79) In direct contrast to No 68922 in the previous frame, 2E Saltley based LMS Class 5 4-6-0 No 44944 is positively gleaming as it simmers in the shed yard at 85C Gloucester (Barnwood) on 30th November 1963. Once of 19A Sheffield (Grimesthorpe), 19C Canklow and 16A Nottingham, No 44944 had been at Saltley shed since November 1959. Between September 1965 and withdrawal in September 1967 it was based at 2B Oxley, 6A Chester and 5B Crewe (South). (N.E.Preedy)

30) As the train it has been giving a helping hand to up the Lickey Incline accelerates away into the distance, BR Class 9F 2-10-0 No 92155, from 21A Saltley and on loan to 85D Bromsgrove, has detached itself at Blackwell station in the summer of 1963. In the right of the picture is another 21A engine, BR Class 9F 2-10-0, No 92157, which is awaiting a path to Bromsgrove with a freight. Both Nos 92155 and 92157 ended their working lives at 8H Birkenhead. (P.A.Bridgman)

1) With the firemen looking towards the camera, BR Class 5 4-6-0 No 73065, of 71A Eastleigh, awaits departure from Southampton (Central) with a through train from Portsmouth & Southsea to Bristol on 5th August 1963. In January 1957, No 73065 was at 19B Millhouses which became part of the Eastern Region in February 1958, being recoded 41C. It arrived on the Southern Region at 71A from 41D Canklow in December 1961. (A.F.Nisbet)

82) Constructed in July 1947, SR Unrebuilt *Battle of Britain* Class 4-6-2 No 34064 *Fighter Command* was modified with a Giesl Oblong Ejector in May 1962, but this fuel saving innovation came too late to save steam on BR from its ultimate decline and extinction. On a soaking wet 30th September 1964, *Fighter Command*, from 70A Nine Elms, is at Waterloo station with the Locomotive Club of Great Britain inspired *'Somerset and Dorset Rail Tour'*. (D.Webster)

83) The yard at 52G Sunderland is all but deserted except for the presence of an enthusiast who is negotiating the tracks and former North Eastern Railway J27 Class 0-6-0 No 65788, a local inhabitant, which is sporting a partially scorched smokebox on 12th December 1964. A once longstanding inhabitant of 51E Stockton, No 65788 was drafted to 51L Thornaby upon the closure of the former shed in June 1959. It was transferred to 52G in March 1962. (N.E.Preedy)

84) At one time a Weymouth locomotive, GWR 1400 Class 0-4-2T No 1453 eventually found its way to 85B Gloucester (Horton Road) in August 1962 via 81B Slough and 84C Banbury. On 27th June 1964, five months before withdrawal and oblivion, No 1453, with a home-made front numberplate, is noted at St.Mary's Crossing Halt, between Stroud and Kemble, with the 1.03pm local passenger from Gloucester. After withdrawal it was cut up at Cashmores, Great Bridge in March 1965. (R.Picton)

85) A month after being reallocated from 67E Dumfries, LMS Hughes Class 6P5F 'Crab' 2-6-0 No 42909 is parked within the confines of its new home at 67C Ayr on 25th July 1964. The 245 units of this useful mixed traffic class were employed at countless depots on many regions of BR and were often employed on holday trains during the summer months. The main purpose of their being based at Ayr shed was to haul the once extensive coal trains in the area. (N.E.Preedy)

86) Bright sunshine envelopes the shed yard at 85B Gloucester (Horton Road) on 10th May 1964. Facing us is locally based GWR 5101 Class 2-6-2T No 5184, for many years an inhabitant of 84D Leamington. Behind No 5184 is GWR *Modified Hall* Class 4-6-0 No 6989 *Wightwick Hall*, another 85B locomotive, destined for withdrawal the following month. After rotting away at Barry Docks for nearly fourteen years, No 6989 was saved for posterity at Quainton Road. (D.K.Jones)

87) Former South Eastern and Chatham Railway N Class 2-6-0 No 31858, from 70C Guildford and in a neglected external condition, steams beneath a lattice-work pedestrian bridge at Reigate and passes the level crossing and signalbox with a three-coach passenger train from Guildford in December 1964. Based for many a year at 73C Hither Green, No 31858 was transferred to 70C in September 1959. Condemned in December 1965 it was scrapped in South Wales. (A.C.Ingram)

88) The photographer has his timing down to perfection as a filthy dirty 62B Dundee Tay Bridge based BR Class 4 2-6-4T emerges from Tayport cutting and is about to disappear from view. No 80124 is in charge of the 6.20am local passenger from Tayport to Dundee on 6th July 1964. The longevity of No 80124's stay at Tay Bridge shed was broken for ever when it was transferred to 64A St.Margarets (Edinburgh) in February 1966, where it died ten months later. (A.F.Nisbet)

89) The exhaust from work-stained LMS *Coronation* Class 4-6-2 No 46254 *City of Stoke-on-Trent*, of 5A Crewe (North), momentarily disturbs the overhead wires as it passes Hartford Junction, between Acton Bridge and Winsford, on 27th June 1964 with the 8.20am express from Carlisle (Citadel) to Birmingham (New Street). Withdrawn from Crewe (North) shed in October 1964, it is hard to believe that this magnificent beast was only eighteen years old. (B.W.L.Brooksbank)

90) Based at 38A/40E Colwick for many a year, former Robinson Great Central Railway 04/7 Class 2-8-0 No 63675 basks in weak sunlight in the yard at Colwick on 10th May 1964. This locomotive was destined to become one of the last active members of the class, being withdrawn from 40E in January 1966. On a visit to the depot by the author on 13th September 1965, Nos 63607, 63644, 63734, 63770 and 63858 were present along with thirty-one other steam types. (N.E.Preedy)

91) A strong wind blows steam sidewards from the safety valves of SR *Merchant Navy* Class 4-6-2 No 35009 *Shaw Savill*, from 83D Exmouth Junction, as it stands near to the imposing coaling plant at 70A Nine Elms in May 1964. At rest beneath the coaling plant is SR Unrebuilt *West Country* Class 4-6-2 No 34105 *Swanage*, of 70F Bournemouth. Withdrawn in September and October 1964 respectively, both were saved by the preservation movement after being dumped at Barry. (A.C.Ingram)

92) Allocated to 82E Bristol Barrow Road in June 1964 after spells at 84E Tyseley, 84G Shrewsbury and 87F Llanelly, BR Class 5 4-6-0 No 73037 finds itself on station pilot duties at Bristol (Temple Meads) on 22nd July 1964, seen here in a section of Brunel's original 1841 station. After a brief foray at 81F Oxford, No 73037 was drafted to the SR in April 1965, firstly to 70D Eastleigh, followed by moves to 70C Guildford and 70A Nine Elms. (H.L.Holland)

93) Beneath an array of upper quadrant signals the fireman of September 1949 constructed SR Rebuilt *West Country Class* 4-6-2 No 34093 *Saunton*, a 70A Nine Elms inmate, swings the bag onto the tender to replenish the water supply at Southampton (Central) station on 18th May 1964. The train *Saunton* is in charge of is the 9.23am excursion from Waterloo to Bournemouth. Note the 'non-regulation' headgear favoured by the Nine Elms firemen at that time. (A.F.Nisbet)

94) Tank engine power dominates the shed scene at 65A Eastfield (Glasgow) on a dull 17th May 1964. From left to right are:- BR Class 4 2-6-4T No 80056, LMS Class 4 2-6-4T No 42690 and sister engine No 42194. All are inmates of 65A at this stage in time. Of the trio, No 42194 was transferred to the North Eastern Region at 56A Wakefield in October 1964. Both Nos 80056 and 42690 were drafted away from Eastfield to 66A Polmadie (Glasgow) in February 1966. (T.R.Amos)

95) Although not officially condemned for a furth two months it is doubtful if 82E Bristol Barrow Road allocated BR Class 5 4-6-0 No 73012 ever turned a wheel in anger again judging by the condition of the right hand cylinder. No 73012, surrounded by former Great Western Railway types, is noted in the shed yard at 82C Swindon on 20th September 1964. Following withdrawal and a period of storage, No 73012 was scrapped at Buttigiegs, Newport in 1965. (Mike Wood)

96) Long since actively preserved at the G.W.S. Centre, Didcot, GWR *Modified Hall* Class 4-6-0 No 6998 *Burton Agnes Hall*, from 81A Old Oak Common, steams into the modern station at Banbury with a down express from Paddington on an overcast day on 23rd April 1964. Once of 86C Cardiff (Canton) and 84G Shrewsbury, No 6998 was allocated to Old Oak Common in January 1961. Prior to withdrawal in December 1965 it was also based at 81C Southall and 81F Oxford. (D.K.Jones)

97) Looking spick and span with its lamp brackets, smokebox hinges, shed and front numberplate spruced-up, former North Eastern Railway J27 Class 0-6-0 No 65814, of 52E Percy Main, is photographed with a brakevan at Newcastle (Central) station on a misty 4th September 1964. When 52E closed in February 1965 it had fifteen of these engines on its books:- Nos 65790/95/96. 65802/5/9/12-14/17/21/25/31/42/58. All were transferred away to other depots. (T.R.Amos)

98) Despite having a slightly scorched smokebox, SR Rebuilt *Battle of Britain* Class 4-6-2 No 34056 *Croydon,* locally based at 83D Exmouth Junction, looks in good external condition at the head of an express at Exeter (St.Davids) station on 2nd August 1964. Constructed in February 1947, *Croydon* was rebuilt at Eastleigh Works in December 1960. Ousted from Exmouth Junction shed in the autumn of 1964, No 34056 found a new haven at 70E Salisbury. (N.E.Preedy)

99) The former London Brighton and South Coast depot at Eastbourne, coded 75G under BR, lost its parent status and allocation in September 1952, becoming a sub-shed of 75A Brighton. Over the years it became run-down, eventually losing its roof, but managed to soldier on until complete closure in June 1965. On 12th July 1964 a quintet of filthy BR Class 4 2-6-4 Tanks, led by No 80153 from 75B Redhill, are in steam in the 'shed' yard. (F.Hornby)

100) With an LMS *Royal Scot* or Rebuilt *Patriot* Class 4-6-0 lurking in the background, BR *Britannia* Class 4-6-2 No 70039 *Sir Christopher Wren*, from 12A Carlisle (Kingmoor), graces the shed yard at 66A Polmadie (Glasgow) on 10th August 1964. Over the years a variety of Pacific types were allocated to Polmadie:- LMS *Princess* and *Coronations*, LNER A2's, BR *Britannias* and *Clans*. The last representatives were A2's Nos 60512/22/24/27/35, withdrawn in 1965. (D.Webster)

101) The 'sharp end' of BR built (1948), but LNER inspired, A2 Class 4-6-2 No 60530 *Sayajirao* is shown to good effect as it faces an unidentified former North British Railway J37 Class in the yard at 62B Dundee Tay Bridge on 28th August 1965. The surviving A2's at Tay Bridge, Nos 60528/30/32, frequently in use as standbys for failed diesels, drew enthusiasts and photographers like magnets to the shed up until their demise at the end of 1966. (N.E.Preedy)

(102) A photographer, hands in pockets, studies GWR *Modified Hall* Class 4-6-0 No 6967 *Willesley Hall*, an 81F Oxford steed, as it pauses at Basingstoke station with an inter-regional express service to Bournemouth on a sunny 17th June 1965. No 6967, paired with a straight-sided tender, is in a very run-down condition with its nameplates having been either stolen or removed for safe-keeping. It was condemned from Oxford shed in December 1965. (N.E.Preedy)

(103) Two more steam engines are seen in deplorable external condition in the shed yard at 70C Guildford on 11th August 1965. Nearest the camera, having attention to a coupling rod, is SR Q1 Class 0-6-0 No 33020, from 70A Nine Elms. To the rear of No 33020 is SR N Class 2-6-0 No 31811, which despite having a well-stocked tender had been withdrawn from Guildford depot the previous month. No 33020, allocated to 70C in November 1965, was condemned in January 1966. (W.G.Piggott)

104) A one time long-term favourite on the books at 52B Heaton in Newcastle, LNER V2 Class 2-6-2 No 60810 was transferred to 50A York in June 1960 and continued to work in revenue earning service from there until taken out of traffic in November 1965. Several months earlier, on 10th July 1965, No 60810 is noted out of steam in the yard at 50A. Placed in storage at York shed until February 1966, No 60810 was despatched to W.George & Son, Wath for scrapping. (N.E.Preedy)

105) SR Unrebuilt *West Country* Class 4-6-2 No 34017 *Ilfracombe* (70D Eastleigh), coaled and watered, basks in the late afternoon sunshine at 70F Bournemouth on Monday, 5th July 1965, awaiting its next rostered turn to Waterloo. Before moving to the South Western Division at 70A Nine Elms in December 1960, *Ilfracombe* was based at 73A Stewarts Lane, 73B Bricklayers Arms and 74B Ramsgate. A final move in June 1966 took No 34017 back to Nine Elms shed. (J.D.Gomersall)

106) Enthusiastic photographers jostle for the best positions whilst others mill around on a platform at Woodford Halse station on 24th April 1965. The subject of this admiration is spruced-up 2F Bescot allocated LMS Class 4F 0-6-0 No 44188 which is in charge of a Stephenson Locomotive Society special. Prior to being based at Bescot in December 1964, No 44188 worked from a variety of sheds, including 18A Toton, 27E Walton, 9G Gorton and 10G Skipton. (B.K.B.Green)

107) Neglected by the cleaning staff at 86B Newport (Ebbw Junction), GWR 2800 Class 2-8-0 No 3864 approaches Gloucester with a fitted freight bound for South Wales on 2nd March 1965. By this date in time these heavy freight workhorses of the Western Region had been much reduced in number by many withdrawals. No 3864 is itself only five months away from condemnation after which it was cut up at Birds, Morriston, Swansea. (N.E.Preedy)

108) With the goods yard at Heathfield all but deserted, BR Class 4 2-6-4T No 80145, from 75B Redhill, departs in a flurry of steam with a Tunbridge Wells West to Eastbourne train on 21st May 1965. The section of line from Eridge to Polegate closed during 1965 along with the intermediate stations at Rotherfield & Mark Cross, Mayfield, Heathfield, Waldron & Horeham Road and Hellingley. Shortly after this picture was taken No 80145 moved to 70E Salisbury. (A.C.Ingram)

109) During the latter years of its lengthy life, GWR 5700 Class 0-6-0PT No 9657 was a firm favourite at Shrewsbury shed, coded 84G, 89A and 6D in British Railways days. On a gloomy 10th February 1965, No 9657 is in a bedgraggled condition stripped of numberplates as it acts on shed pilot duties at Shrewsbury. No 9657 was destined to survive at Shrewsbury depot until April 1966. Following withdrawal it was disposed of at Cashmores, Great Bridge. (D.K.Jones)

10) Once of 65F Grangemouth for many years, LMS Hughes Class 6P5F 'Crab' 2-6-0 No 42737 was reallocated to 67C Ayr in January 1961. Although out of steam in the shed yard at Ayr on 21st August 1965, No 42737 looks in fine external fettle in a line-up of locomotives. Officially condemned in December 1966, No 42737 was noted in store at 65J Stirling until around March 1967 when it was despatched for scrapping at Campbells yard at Airdrie. (N.E.Preedy)

11) Designed between 1889 and 1923 by Adams, with some modifications by Drummond, the SR 02 Class 0-4-4 Tanks were mostly employed on branch line work. By January 1957 there were thirty-seven of them still at work, including nineteen examples on the Isle of Wight where they were a spotters delight hauling their antiquated coaches until late in 1966. The long preserved No 24 *Calbourne* (70H Ryde) is seen at Ryde Pier station on 25th September 1965. (Alan Jones)

112) Their days of revenue earning service gone for ever, two condemned locomotives stand cold and lifeless as they await the inevitable at 81C Southall on 21st February 1965. For GWR 4500 Class 2-6-2T No 5569 it is a far cry from the days it was employed on branch trains in Devon and Cornwall when allocated to 83D Laira (Plymouth). Behind No 5569 is GWR *Castle* Class 4-6-0 No 7013 *Bristol Castle*. Both were scrapped at Cox & Danks, Park Royal. (M.S.Stokes)

113) The final member of the BR Class 5 4-6-0's, No 73171, of 70D Eastleigh, rattles a Salisbury bound freight past Worting Junction, near Basingstoke, on 3rd April 1965. Released into traffic in May 1957, No 73171 was initially allocated to 50A York. It remained on the North Eastern Region until September 1963, working from 55A Leeds (Holbeck) and 55D Royston. Withdrawn from Eastleigh shed in October 1966 it was cut up at Cashmores, Newport in 1967. (Ken Ellis)

14) Its soot-stained smokebox partially scorched, 52G Sunderland based former North Eastern Railway Q6 Class 0-8-0 No 63410 leaks steam as it passes West Hartlepool shed (51C) light engine on a bright early autumn day in October 1965. After many years of being a 51C locomotive, No 63410 had been at Sunderland depot since April 1965. Condemned from the latter in June 1966 it was scrapped at Hughes Bolckows Ltd., North Blyth a month later. (N.E.Preedy)

15) A *'cop'* for the photographer. Begrimed LMS Class 5 4-6-0 No 45236, of 12A Carlisle (Kingmoor), is a visitor to 64A St.Margarets (Edinburgh) on Sunday, 13th July 1965, where it is seen in steam near to the antiquated coaling stage and an unidentified LNER B1 Class 4-6-0. Once of Barrow shed, No 45236 served at both Carlisle (Kingmoor) and Upperby sheds from November 1959 until withdrawn from the former upon closure in December 1967. (Ken Ellis)

116) The fireman of BR Class 9F 2-10-0 No 92087 takes a well-earned breather as his mount, looking in respectable condition, basks in sunshine on a centre road at Gloucester (Central) on 16th July 1965. No 92087 is in charge of a rake of empty iron-ore tippers belonging to Northamptonshire Iron-Ore Mines. Although 2D Banbury is stencilled on the smokebox door, No 92087 had just been transferred from Banbury to Northampton shed, coded 1H. (N.E.Preedy)

117) By the autumn of 1965 the old Somerset and Dorset Railway was in its death throes and the weeds are taking over at Glastonbury station on 3rd September as LMS Ivatt Class 2 2-6-2T No 41249, of 83G Templecombe, sets off under clear signals with the 2.52pm local train bound for Evercreech Junction, consisting of a single coach and a covered wagon. In common with the majority of the S & D system, Glastonbury closed completely in early March 1966. (R.Picton)

18) Although fully coaled and apparently in good working order, December 1941 constructed SR Rebuilt *Merchant Navy* Class 4-6-2 No 35005 *Canadian Pacific* (70G Weymouth) is only two months away from withdrawal as it poses for the camera in bright sunshine on the coaling road at 70A Nine Elms on 13th August 1965. *Canadian Pacific* was transported to Barry Docks in April 1966 where it stayed until saved by the preservation movement in March 1973. (D.K.Jones)

19) Like the finger-less clock on the apex of the shed roof at 66E Carstairs, life is almost time-expired for locally based LMS Class 5 4-6-0 No 44973 which is seen in steam on a dead-end road on 3rd June 1965. Once one of a batch of numerically sequenced engines allocated to 65J/63B Fort William (Nos 44972-77), this locomotive was transferred to 66A Polmadie (Glasgow) in December 1961. Allocated to Carstairs in May 1963 it was condemned in September 1965. (D.Webster)

120) Only allocated to three sheds between January 1957 and August 1964, Bristol Barrow Road, Shrewsbury and Chester, LMS *Jubilee* Class 4-6-0 No 45660 *Rooke* found itself on the books at 55A Leeds (Holbeck) in September 1964. Nearing the end of its career it exudes sulphurous exhaust fumes as it takes on fresh supplies beneath the coaling plant at Holbeck depot in the early spring of 1966. Withdrawn in June 1966, *Rooke* was cut up at Drapers, Hull. (R.Butterfield)

21) Looking the worse for wear, BR Class 4 2-6-0 No 76010, from 70F Bournemouth, departs from Wareham station (change for Swanage) with a two-coach local passenger train bound for Weymouth on 30th July 1966. An Eastleigh locomotive for many years, except for a brief foray at 72C Yeovil between September 1958 and January 1961, No 76010 was allocated to Bournemouth shed in October 1965. It was rendered redundant from the same in September 1966. (W.G.Piggott)

22) An enthusiast, dressed in the attire of the day, peers curiously into the cab of SR USA Class 0-6-0T No 30064 as it rests between duties as a works pilot at Eastleigh on 2nd April 1966. Between August and September of this same year, No 30064 was loaned out to Meldon Quarry before returning to 70D Eastleigh. Constructed by the Vulcan Foundry in the USA in 1943, No 30064 was withdrawn in July 1967. It is now on the Bluebell Railway. (F.Hornby)

123) The pioneer member of the Peppercorn inspired LNER K1 Class 2-6-0's first introduced into service in 1949, No 62001, locally based at 51C, trundles past the depot light engine on 5th June 1966. Being a modern design the K1's were not affected by withdrawals until 1963 and many continued in service until steam on the North Eastern Region finished in late 1967. No 62001, posted to 50A York in February 1967, was condemned two months later. (D.K.Jones)

124) Cleaned up specially for the occasion, two 62A Thornton Junction based former North British Railway J37 Class 0-6-0's Nos 64570 and 64618 join forces to haul the Warwickshire Railway Society Railtour, *The Aberdonian*, on 25th June 1966. The special is seen at Alloa station, where a photo-stop was made. Both engines were withdrawn towards the end of 1966 and were scrapped at Campbells, Airdrie and the Motherwell Machinery Co, Wishaw respectively. (N.E.Preedy)

125) Although of Great Western Railway vintage and coded 84C by the Western Region authorities, Banbury shed, taken over by the LMR in 1963 (2D), had, by 26th February 1966, lost its allocation of former GWR engines, being replaced by LMS ones, notably Class 5 4-6-0's and Class 8F 2-8-0's. In this scene all of the locomotives on view are of the LMS variety, with the exception of BR Class 9F 2-10-0 No 92212, itself an 84C engine earlier in its career. (D.K.Jones)

126) Locally based BR *Britannia* Class 4-6-2 No 70009 *Alfred the Great* is out of action outside the running shed at 12A Carlisle (Kingmoor) in the summer of 1966 awaiting repair. On an adjacent track is BR Class 9F 2-10-0 No 92076, another inhabitant of Kingmoor. The writing was on the wall for both of these engines with condemnation looming on the horizon. *Alfred the Great* was destined to be a victim of the cutter's torch at McWilliams, Shettleston. (D.K.Jones)

127) It is the 26th September 1966 and there is not a Southern locomotive in sight in a section of the yard near to some goods sidings at 70A Nine Elms. In the centre of the frame a dead BR Class 3 2-6-2T No 82023 is shunted by BR Class 4 2-6-4T No 80143, both inhabitants of Nine Elms. Behind the tank engines is BR Class 5 4-6-0 No 73110 *The Red Knight*, from 70C Guildford. Of the three, only No 80143 survived until the end of steam on the Southern. (W.G.Piggott)

128) SR *Merchant Navy* Class 4-6-2 No 35030 *Elder Dempster Lines*, a 70G Weymouth engine since September 1964, heads the LCGB 'Great Central Rail Tour' on 3rd September 1966, seen here making tracks at Newton to the north of Rugby GC. Built in April 1949, No 35030 was rebuilt at Eastleigh Works in April 1958. Based for much of its life at 70A Nine Elms, *Elder Dempster Lines* returned to the same from Weymouth in March 1967, four months prior to withdrawal. (W.G.Piggott)

29) The noise must have been excrutiating as two sets of safety valves are lifted on LMS Class 4 2-6-4 Tanks, Nos 42644 and 42574 at Blaneau Ffestiniog station on 24th September 1966. Both locomotives are from 9E Trafford Park and involved in the haulage of an enthusiasts special. No 42574 was drafted to the North Eastern Region at 56A Wakefield in November 1966 and survived until October 1967. No 42644 was withdrawn in March 1967 from 9E. (B.K.B.Green)

30) A trio of locomotives are in steam in the shed yard at 62B Dundee Tay Bridge on a soaking wet day in May 1966. In the left of the picture is LNER A2 Class 4-6-2 No 60532 *Blue Peter*, behind which is an unidentified LNER B1 Class 4-6-0. In the right of the frame is A2 Class 4-6-2 No 60528 *Tudor Minstrel*. The subsequent preservation and exploits of *Blue Peter* are well recorded, whereas *Tudor Minstrel* died a lonely death at McWilliams, Shettleston in October 1966. (N.E.Preedy)

131) LMS Class 3F 'Jinty' 0-6-0T No 47658, employed as shunter No 6, is in deplorable external condition as it passes Flag Lane signalbox at Crewe Works with a single low-loader on 3rd October 1966. This must have been one of the last operational duties for No 47658 as Crewe Works ceased its long association with steam shunters during this same month. Once of 5F Uttoxeter and 5D Stoke, No 47658 began its career at Crewe Works in February 1962. (D.K.Jones)

132) Work-stained LNER B1 Class 4-6-0 No 61021 *Reitbok*, stripped of nameplates, is a visitor to Mirfield depot from 50A York on 6th December 1966. Prior to being allocated to 50A in September 1960, *Reitbok* had been an inmate of 51A Darlington (twice), 51G Haverton Hill, 51L Thornaby and 56A Wakefield. Mirfield shed, of Lancashire & Yorkshire Railway origin, owned by both the LMR and NER authorities and coded 25D & 56D, closed to steam on 2nd January 1967. (N.E.Preedy)

133) 70E Salisbury based BR Class 4 2-6-0 No 76007 pays a visit to 70D Eastleigh where it stands in the yard in steam on 5th July 1966. Itself an Eastleigh engine in 1957, No 76007 was drafted to a new home at 71B Bournemouth in May 1958, moving to Salisbury the following month. A final transfer back to Bournemouth shed occurred in April 1967, three months before withdrawal and oblivion at the hands of Birds, Risca in November 1967. (J.D.Gomersall)

134) Whilst on the subject of Bournemouth we find ourselves at the station on 30th March 1966 where we espy SR Rebuilt *West Country* Class 4-6-2 No 34009 *Lyme Regis* (70D Eastleigh) blowing off excess steam at the head of a rake of Southern coaching stock. Although the station itself is much the same today, the semaphore signalling, motive power depot and through tracks are long gone, as is *Lyme Regis*, withdrawn from 70A Nine Elms in October 1966. (N.E.Preedy)

135) Gently lifting its safety valves, BR Class 4 4-6-0 No 75029, from 6D Shrewsbury, takes refreshment from a water column at Welshpool station on 24th September 1966. No 75029, modified with a double chimney in May 1957, is coupled to another BR Standard type. This engine worked from a variety of sheds from 1957 until withdrawal and preservation at the East Somerset Railway in the late sixties, including 81F Oxford, 27C Southport and 82C Swindon. (Ken Ellis)

136) As two track workers make their way along the permanent way, 51C West Hartlepool based former North Eastern Railway Q6 Class 0-8-0 No 63407 leaks steam as it is about to overtake them with a heavy freight train at Greetham on 3rd June 1966. Once of 51G Haverton Hill, 51F West Auckland and 51A Darlington, No 63407 had been at West Hartlepool depot since April 1964. Taken out of traffic in July 1967 it was cut up at Clayton & Davie, Dunston-on-Tyne. (T.R.Amos)

137) For many years a North Eastern Region locomotive based at 55C Farnley Junction, 55F Manningham (Bradford) and 55E Normanton, LMS Hughes Class 6P5F 'Crab' 2-6-0 No 42702 was drafted to Scotland to 67C Ayr in November 1963 where it was employed on freight trains, mostly of the mineral variety, until condemnation in January 1966. On Tuesday, 23rd August 1966, it lies unwanted in the yard at Ayr in the company of a BR Class 4 2-6-0. (A.C.Ingram)

138) Although Carlisle (Kingmoor) had a massive allocation over the years, very few of the LMS Class 8F 2-8-0's were actually on its books, but there were plenty of visitors from other depots, including No 48252, from 6C Croes Newywdd, seen in steam at 12A on 7th October 1966 in the company of LMS Class 5 4-6-0 No 45299, of 5D Stoke. No 48252 worked from 5B Crewe (South) and 9F Heaton Mersey sheds before being rendered surplus to requirements in May 1968. (N.E.Preedy)

139) Sidings in the distance are packed with wagons of all descriptions as uncared-for SR Rebuilt *West Country* Class 4-6-2 No 34018 *Axminster*, from 70A Nine Elms, departs light engine from Brockenhurst in a flurry of steam and heads for Bournemouth on 19th April 1967. By this date steam workings were few and far between on the Southern and within a matter of weeks was to disappear completely. *Axminster* drew its fire for the last time early in July 1967. (W.G.Piggott)

40) Although the former North British Railway depot at 64A St.Margarets had closed completely on 22nd April 1967 it housed a solitary LMS Class 5 4-6-0 No 44997, ex. 63A Perth, withdrawn in May 1967, for use as a stationary boiler at Craigentinny carriage sidings for steam heating purposes until July 1967. On the 11th of the same month, No 44997 is seen in steam by the side of the defunct running shed. It was scrapped two months later. (S.Turnbull)

41) Its life's work completed, LNER B1 Class 4-6-0 No 61035 *Pronghorn,* stripped of plates and condemned in December 1966, awaits its fate at 50A York on 15th January 1967. For many years a 50B/55H Leeds (Neville Hill) steed, *Pronghorn* arrived at 50A via 52C Blaydon, 52B Heaton and 52A Gateshead. It was disposed of at Drapers, Hull in May 1967. York shed, once a bastion of steam, losts its allocation of the same in July 1967, becoming a diesel depot. (D.K.Jones)

142) As 1967 progressed more and more steam depots either closed completely or became dieselised and at the remaining sheds in many cases withdrawn locomotives outnumbered the living ones. In August 1967, LMS Fairburn Class 4 2-6-4T No 42297 is stored lifeless at the side of 10D Lostock Hall's running shed after condemnation three months earlier. In happier times, No 42297 had been actively employed from the sheds at Wigan L & Y and Patricroft. (D.K.Jones)

143) Nine of the robust SR USA Class 0-6-0 Tanks survived into 1967, from the sheds at Eastleigh and Guildford and also in Departmental stock. No 30071 stands out of steam outside Eastleigh depot, the roof of which is deteriorating rapidly, on 25th March 1967. Although long since demolished, the former running lines within the former shed remained in situ for many years after closure. No 30071 met its fate at Cashmores, Newport in March 1968. (D.K.Jones)

44) Conversation time at Preston on 29th July 1967, where steam triumphs over diesel traction. LMS Class 5 4-6-0 No 45000, from the nearby shed at 10D Lostock Hall, is coupled to a failed English Electric Type 3 No D6754 which 'was' in charge of a Saturdays Only express from Blackpool to Newcastle. Although withdrawn three months later, No 45000 was preserved as part of the National collection and is based on the Severn Valley Railway. (N.E.Preedy)

45) High pressure steam trails behind former North Eastern Railway J27 Class 0-6-0 No 65892 as it heads bunker-first for home at Sunderland down the Silkworth branch with a fully-laden coal train from Silkworth Colliery on 15th June 1967. Allocated to Sunderland shed for many years, punctuated by brief spells at 51L Thornaby and 52F Blyth, No 65892 was withdrawn in August 1967. Scrapping came at the hands of Willoughbys, Choppington four months later. (N.E.Preedy)

146) Especially 'bulled-up' for the occasion, 5B Crewe (South) allocated LMS Class 5 4-6-0 No 44680 is noted near the carriage sidings at Tyseley on 5th March 1967 with a Stephenson Locomotive Society special bound for Wolverhampton (Low Level) and Shrewsbury. Although Tyseley shed 'officially' closed to steam on 7th November 1966 it continued to play host to many steam engines from areas of the London Midland Region for wheel turning purposes. (Mike Wood)

147) Fully coaled, work-stained LMS Class 8F 2-8-0 No 48045, once of Northwich (twice), Toton, Widnes (twice), Mold Junction, Speke Junction, Warrington, Nottingham, Westhouses and Kirkby, stands in the yard of its last home at 8A Edge Hill (Liverpool) in the company of sister engine No 48268, another 8A engine, on a dull 27th August 1967. The latter was condemned from Edge Hill two months later, but No 48045 soldiered on until the shed closed in May 1968. (R.Picton)

48) For the spotter on foot the twenty minute walk from the nearest station to the depot at Tyne Dock was well worth it even in the latter days of steam at the shed with its dilapidated roundhouses, straight running structure and spacious workshop. Towards the end of its long life former NER Q6 Class 0-8-0 No 63426 is noted in bright sunlight in a corner of one of the roofless roundhouses on 11th June 1967, a month before withdrawal. (N.E.Preedy)

49) Possibly substituting for a Bulleid Pacific, BR Class 5 4-6-0 No 73092, from 70C Guildford and in disgraceful external condition minus number and shedplates, thunders through Weybridge station with the 08.46 Bournemouth (Central) to Waterloo express on 28th March 1967. From January 1957 until condemnation in July 1967, No 73092 worked on three regions of BR, the LMR, WR and SR, including the depots at Patricroft, Shrewsbury, Gloucester and Eastleigh. (D.K.Jones)

150) Ex. NER J27 Class 0-6-0 No 65789, a new arrival at 52G Sunderland from 52F Blyth, sports a scorched smokebox as it passes beneath a signal gantry near to some weed-strewn tracks at Ryehope Junction with a short mineral train on a bright 12th June 1967. At one time there were two stations near to Ryehope Junction - Ryhope, closed in 1953 and Ryhope East, closed in 1960. The depot at Sunderland closed to steam in September 1967. (N.E.Preedy)

151) Although bereft of nameplates, BR *Britannia* Class 4-6-2 No 70011 *Hotspur*, of 12A Carlisle (Kingmoor), still looks every inch an express passenger locomotive as it graces the yard at 5B Crewe (South) on a sunny 2nd June 1967. Once part of the stud of *Britannias* allocated to 32A Norwich, *Hotspur* found its way to Carlisle in December 1963, via 31B March. It was employed from both Kingmoor and Upperby until its demise from the former in December 1967. (N.E.Preedy)

52) Bric-a-brac associated with railway depots is scattered about in the yard outside the roundhouses at 55A Leeds (Holbeck) where one of the last active LMS Class 4 2-6-4 Tanks, No 42145, is parked near to a large puddle in July 1967. A one time Scottish Region locomotive at Carstairs shed, No 42145 had been drafted to the North Eastern Region at 56B Ardsley in October 1963. It was transferred to 56F Low Moor in August 1967 from Holbeck. (R.Butterfield)

53) Minus nameplates SR Rebuilt *West Country* Class 4-6-2 No 34036 *Westward* Ho, of 70A Nine Elms, is reduced to hauling a ballast train at Clapham Junction on a dull 6th May 1967. Built in July 1946, *Westward Ho* was rebuilt at Eastleigh Works in August 1960. Earlier in its career it was housed at 72D Plymouth (Friary), 72A Exmouth Junction, 70E Salisbury and 70D Eastleigh. Withdrawn in July 1967 it was later scrapped at Cashmores, Newport in 1968. (J.M.Gascoyne)

154) A 350 hp 0-6-0 diesel performs on shunting duties as 8E Northwich based LMS Class 8F 2-8-0 No 48735 rounds the curve from the Chester direction and passes the site of 5A Crewe (North) with a train of up mineral wagons on 16th June 1967. No 48735 was a Western Region locomotive for many years, working from the depots at 87K Swansea (Victoria) and 87F Llanelly. It was sent to the LMR in September 1964, initially to 10D Lostock Hall. (Christopher Fifield)

155) A summer extra sees a trainload of holidaymakers returning home to the drudgery of their everyday lives as LMS Class 5 4-6-0 No 45226, from 10D Lostock Hall, sets off for Manchester from Blackpool (North) on 8th July 1967. Ousted from 24A Accrington in April 1960, No 45226 found a new home at 24F Fleetwood where it remained until drafted to Lostock Hall in July 1963. Condemned in September 1967 it was stored for a while prior to being cut up in 1968. (Christopher Fifield)

156) Dwarfed by a massive modern power station, a line-up of redundant steam locomotives are stored in the closed shed yard at 56A Wakefield on a warm-looking 9th July 1967. In the extreme left of the frame is a WD Class 8F 2-8-0. Parked together are three BR Class 9F 2-10-0's, two of which can be identified as Nos 92065 and 92030. The former, condemned in April 1967, was a 52H Tyne Dock steed until being transferred to Wakefield in November 1966. (R.Butterfield)

157) 'Live' BR Class 9F 2-10-0's abound in the shed yard at 8H Birkenhead on a sun-filled 6th May 1967. From left to right are No 92167 (a once long-term resident of 21A Saltley and fitted with a Berkeley mechanical stoker), 92089 (once part of a large fleet of such engines based at Annesley shed) and former Crosti-boilered No 92023 (a former inmate of 15A Wellingborough). On 6th November 1967 Birkenhead closed to steam and the depot was much reduced in importance. (N.E.Preedy)

158) With the distant signal clearing a through path, BR *Britannia* Class 4-6-2 No 70013 *Oliver Cromwell* and LMS Class 5 4-6-0 No 44871, both from 10A Carnforth and in immaculate condition, combine to double-head a Locomotive Club of Great Britain sponsored special near to Sough tunnel on 4th August 1968. After withdrawal both engines were destined for preservation, *Oliver Cromwell* at Bressingham and No 44871 at Steamtown, Carnforth. (T.R.Amos)

159) With the end of steam on the horizon a member of the footplate crew of LMS Class 8F 2-8-0 No 48168 contemplates what is possibly a bleak future as his charge is rotated on the turntable at 9K Bolton in late May 1968. Although bearing the stencilled lettering of 9F Heaton Mersey on the smokebox door, No 48168 had been transferred to Bolton the same month. Despite this stay of execution it was withdrawn the following month. (Christopher Fifield)

160) By the beginning of 1968 very few individual classes were left to represent the dying days of steam and in the main it was representatives of the LMS 4-6-0 and 8F 2-8-0 wheel arrangements that carried the flag. On a bright 2nd February 1968, Class 5 4-6-0 No 44878, still carrying its numberplate, throws smoke into the crisp air at 10D Lostock Hall. A longstanding inmate of 12A Carlisle (Kingmoor), No 44878 had been drafted to 10D in January 1968. (N.E.Preedy)

161) With grim-looking back-to-back style dwellings in the right of the picture, locally based LMS Class 5 4-6-0 No 44781 passes Bolton shed light engine in the spring of 1968. When 9J Agecroft closed completely on 17th October 1966 this longstanding resident was reallocated to 9E Trafford Park. Apart from Bolton, No 44781 also worked from Newton Heath and Carnforth sheds until condemned in August 1968 and later took an active role in the 'Virgin Soldiers'. (Christopher Fifield)

162) Given the pace of modernisation during the sixties it is amazing that some pockets of regular steam hauled expresses survived until 1968. Looking generally unkempt and leaking steam from many locations, 10D Lostock Hall based LMS Class 5 4-6-0 No 45444 sets off from Preston station with the 12.44pm express for Blackpool on 16th April 1968. Withdrawn at the end of BR steam, No 45444 was scrapped at Drapers, Hull after a period of storage at 10D. (R.Picton)

163) Allocated to 10A Carnforth following a move from 10J Lancaster (Green Ayre) in April 1966, LMS Class 5 4-6-0 No 45025 simmers gently on the northern turntable at 9D Newton Heath on a bright 21st April 1968. Once of 1A Willesden and 12B Carlisle (Upperby), No 45025 was another member of the class to work until the end of steam. Following condemnation it was immediately earmarked for active preservation on the Strathspey Railway, Aviemore. (N.E.Preedy)

164) A line-up of redundant and lifeless locomotives are parked on a dead-road in the yard at 10A Carnforth on 3rd June 1968. Although not officially withdrawn from service until August 1968 it is doubtful if the leading engine, BR Class 4 4-6-0 No 75020, equipped with a double chimney, was ever steamed again. A one-time Western Region engine at 89A Oswestry, 84E Tyseley, 89C Machynlleth and 89B Croes Newyd it was scrapped in November 1968 at a yard in Airdrie. (C.P.Stacey)

165) The former Lancashire & Yorkshire Railway owned shed at Normanton, coded 20D and 55E by the LMR and NER authorities, closed in the autumn of 1967 and in this picture taken on Sunday, 18th February 1968, we can capture a small part of what the inside of a steam shed looked like. Amidst the ghostly silence, awaiting their turn to be towed away for scrap, are two LMS Class 4 2-6-4 Tanks, an LMS Class 4 'Flying Pig' 2-6-0 and an LNER B1 Class 4-6-0. (A.C.Ingram)

166) Looking in fine external fettle and with a freight special (8X46) chalked on the top of its smokebox door, resident LMS Class 5 4-6-0 No 45381 stands next to sister locomotive, No 45104, in the shed yard at 9K Bolton in the spring of 1968. Despite its superb condition, No 45381 was withdrawn from Bolton in May 1968, followed by No 45104 in June 1968. They were cut up at Wards, Killamarsh and Cohens, Kettering respectively in 1968 and 1969. (Christopher Fifield)

167) The final passenger train rostered for steam haulage when the end came on 11th August 1968 was the 'fifteen guinea' special from Liverpool to Manchester, Manchester to Carlisle and return utilising three LMS Class 5 4-6-0's Nos 44781, 44871, 45110 and BR *Britannia* Class 4-6-2 No 70013 *Oliver Cromwell*. In this picture, No 45110, from 10D Lostock Hall, passes Type 2 diesel No D7634 on a freight, as it departs from Rainhill station. (T.R.Amos)

168) Spruced-up in readiness to power an enthusiasts special, locally based LMS Class 5 4-6-0 No 45390 lets off steam in the shed yard at 10A Carnforth on 4th August 1968. Once of 5A Crewe (North), 5B Crewe (South), 5D Stoke, 6J Holyhead (twice), 6B Mold Junction and 8A Edge Hill (Liverpool), No 45390 had been a regular at Carnforth since June 1962. After dropping its fire for the last time it was stored briefly at Carnforth before being despatched for a final sad journey to Drapers, Hull for cutting up. (W.G.Piggott)

169) 'C' Shop at Swindon Works was always busy with a constant stream of steam locomotives arriving for cutting up. On the occasion of an official tour on 12th August 1962, GWR 5600 Class 0-6-2T No 5682, late of 88E Abercynon (May 1962), is in various stages of being dismantled having lost its cab and buffers. To the left of No 5682 are several locos awaiting the same fate and in the right of the frame is GWR 5700 Class 0-6-0PT No 5758. (N.L.Browne)

170) Waiting their turn to be scrapped on 18th April 1963 at Cashmores, Great Bridge are LMS Class 3 2-6-2T No 40104 and LMS Class 3F 0-6-0T No 47479, both ex. 2B Nuneaton, LMS Class 4 2-6-4 Tanks Nos 42362 and 42323, ex. 5D Stoke, LNER B1 Class 4-6-0's Nos 61139 and 61151, ex. 41A Sheffield (Darnall), LNER K3 Class 2-6-0 No 61960 (40B Immingham), LMS Class 3 2-6-2T No 40115 (16B Kirkby) and LMS Class 3F 0-6-0T No 47381 (24J Lancaster - Green Ayre). (T.R.Amos)

71) There were a number of scrapyards in and around the Sheffield area and awaiting entry to Wards yard in Beighton on 8th February 1966 are BR Class 5 4-6-0 No 73036 (6D Shrewsbury), LMS Class 8F 2-8-0 No 48094 (6B Mold Junction) and GWR *Modified Hall* Class 4-6-0 No 6964 *Thornbridge Hall* (2D Banbury), all of which were condemned in September 1965. Also present is LMS Class 6P5F 2-6-0 No 42947, withdrawn from 9F Heaton Mersey in December 1965. (A.Wakefield)

72) An infamous British Railways scrapyard in the north-east was an offshoot of Darlington Works where forlorn lines of engines silently awaited the cutter's torch. On 13th May 1962, still in one piece, are LNER J72 0-6-0T No 68688, late of 51D Middlesbrough, 51L Thornaby (twice) and 51F West Auckland, condemned in October 1961 and sister locomotive No 68703, also condemned in October 1961, from 51C West Hartlepool. (H.N.James)

173) SR *Schools* Class 4-4-0 No 3092 *Stowe*, for many years an inmate a 73B Bricklayers Arms, was withdraw from 75A Brighton in November 196 and was eventually actively restore for service on the Bluebell Railway. O 26th May 1963 it is seen in the yar outside the running shed at 75D Stewar Lane. (T.R.Amos)

174) LNER Gresley V2 Class 2-6-2 No 60800 *Green Arrow* was, for some, unexpectedly withdrawn from 34A Kings Cross in August 1962. Reserved as part of the National Collection at York, *Green Arrow* was restored to active service. On 10th June 1973 it is seen approaching Henley in Arden with a special. (T.R.Amos)

175) A unique occasion on the Sever Valley Railway with the triple-headin of GWR 5700 Class 0-6-0 Pannier Tank on 25th September 1993. Departin from Bewdley station with th 9.35am Bridgnorth to Kidderminster ar Nos 7714 (a former NCBengine), 576 and 5775, (formerly belonging t London Transport). (R.W.Hinton)